The Tarantula

A Dillon Remarkable Animals Book

The Tarantula

By Gail LaBonte

Dillon Press
New York

Acknowledgments

My sincerest gratitude goes to Rick C. West of the Royal British Columbia Museum in Victoria, B.C., for his assistance in providing information, range maps, many excellent photographs, and for checking the manuscript for accuracy. I owe thanks for photographs and information to: Chip Clark of the Smithsonian Insect Zoo; Frederick A. Coyle; Georgia Eddy of the Arizona-Sonora Desert Museum; Sally Love of the Smithsonian Insect Zoo; Rick McIntyre; Allen McKee; Al Morgan; Thomas R. Prentice; and Dr. Edward S. Ross.

Library of Congress Cataloging-in-Publication Data

LaBonte, Gail.
   The tarantula / by Gail LaBonte.
      p.   cm.— (A Dillon remarkable animals book)
   Summary: Examines the physical characteristics, habits, natural environment, and bad reputation of this large, hairy spider.
   ISBN 0-382-39235-3 pbk 0-87518-452-9 hc
   1. Tarantulas—Juvenile literature. [1. Tarantulas.
   2. Spiders.] I. Title. II. Series.
   QL458.42.T5L33   1991
   595.4′4—dc20   90-45773
                                            CIP
                                            AC

Macmillan Publishing Company, 866 Third Avenue
New York, NY 10022

Printed in the United States of America
   3 4 5 6 7 8 9 10 hc

1 2 3 4 5 6 7 8 9 10 pbk

Contents

Facts about the Tarantula

Scientific Name: *Theraphosidae*

Description:

Length of Body—Less than 1 inch to as long as 4 inches (less than 2.5 to 10 centimeters)

Leg Span—Less than 2 inches to as long as 10.5 inches (less than 5 to 26.3 centimeters)

Weight—As much as 4.4 ounces (123.2 grams)

Physical Features—Large and hairy fangs point down; long pedipalps; eight eyes; two spinnerets

Color—Light brown to black, also blue-gray; some have yellow or red sections; some are one color; other have stripes and patterns

Distinctive Habits: Some species dig burrows in ground; others live in trees and build silk tubes in hollow trunks or among leaves; all species kill prey with poison that flows through fangs; do not see well; scientists are not certain if they can smell or hear

Food: Mainly insects, such as beetles and crickets; also lizards, frogs, small snakes, baby birds, and small rodents

Reproduction: Females of some species mature in 2 to 3 years; others mature in 10 to 12 years; males travel to find mates; females lay 100 to 1000 eggs and keep them in a silk cocoon; eggs hatch in about 4 to 6 weeks

Life Span: 2 to 28 years

Range: Australia, New Guinea; Indonesia, and southern Asia;
   Africa and Middle East except for extremely dry regions;
   South America except for southern halves of Argentina
   and Chile; Caribbean islands except for Jamaica; Central
   America; Mexico; and southwestern United States

The shaded areas on this map show the range of the tarantula.

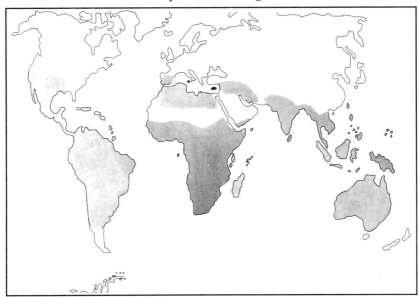

Giant Spiders

Long ago in Taranto, a small town in Italy, the people enjoyed dancing to lively music at their village's many festivals. Perhaps because they spent so much time celebrating and not enough time working, the government passed a law against dancing.

The people of Taranto did not want to give up their fun. Instead, they invented a story about a big spider that was often seen near their town. They said the only way to survive this spider's bite was to dance wildly enough to sweat out its deadly poison.

Soon, the villagers were dancing again. Over time, this dance came to be called the *tarantella,*

Giant spiders, such as this Malaysian tarantula, have been frightening people for centuries.

and the spider became known as the tarantula.

The villagers had a good time fooling the government with their trick. However, the poor spider never lost its reputation for being scary. When explorers from Europe reached the New World, they were frightened by the even larger spiders they found there. They called these spiders "tarantulas," too, and the name stuck.

Surprisingly, the spider of Taranto, Italy, is not closely related to the spiders that modern-day scientists call tarantulas. The Italian creature is really a wolf spider. Like a real wolf, it travels away from its home, hunting for food. A wolf spider is big but looks tame compared to the hairy giants now known as tarantulas.

Scary but Shy

The giant spiders of the New World looked very dangerous to the European explorers centuries ago. Like these explorers, many people today

A wolf spider.

wonder how dangerous tarantulas really are.

People do not need to worry about tarantulas. They don't usually attack animals larger than themselves. The bite of a tarantula is poisonous enough to kill insects, lizards, frogs, baby birds, and small rodents, but not humans.

Sometimes, people who handle these spiders are bitten. They say the bites are no worse than bee stings. But a few people have rare allergies. Bee stings can make them very sick, and the tarantula's **venom***, or poison, can too. Its bite could be very dangerous and even deadly for these people. Though this is rare, it is best for everyone to avoid being bitten, since the spider's bite is painful and and might become infected.

Even if a tarantula's venom is not dangerous, its size alone is enough to frighten people. Tarantulas are the largest spiders in the world. In the United States, the bodies of adults are from 1 to 3 inches (2.5 to 7.5 centimeters) long. Their legs make them look even larger.

According to the *Guinness Book of World Records*, the largest spider ever measured was a Goliath bird-eater, a South American **species**, or kind, of tarantula. This giant had a leg span of 10.5 inches (26.3 centimeters). Its body was 4 inches

*Words in **bold type** are explained in the glossary at the end of this book.

The Goliath bird-eater is the largest species of tarantula. This Goliath bird-eater is eating a rat.

(10 centimeters) long and weighed 4.4 ounces (123.2 grams)—more than a quarter of a pound!

Because of their remarkable size, tarantulas have held some unusual jobs. Some even work as actors in Hollywood! In a Hollywood movie, *Arachnophobia*—which means "fear of spiders,"

—a town is taken over by "deadly" tarantulas. Although real tarantulas acted in the movie, the filmmakers built a mechanical spider for the more frightening scenes. They did this because they couldn't make the real tarantulas act fierce enough.

Other tarantulas work as security guards inside jewelry cases. This keeps thieves' fingers out! Jewelry store owners hope that burglars won't know how harmless the creatures really are.

Although they look alarming, most tarantulas are shy creatures. They are **nocturnal,** or active at night, so people don't see them very often. This makes them even more startling when they appear. Many people fear spiders, and spiders as large as these are an amazing sight.

Eight-Legged Pets

Tarantulas are not only the largest and heaviest spiders, they also live longer than other spiders. Females of some species live as long as 20 years.

Most tarantulas—such as this Thailand tarantula hiding in its burrow—are shy creatures.

Males of the same species usually live 10 or 12 years. One record-holding tarantula lived to be 28-years-old! These spiders' long lives help make them attractive as pets.

Tarantulas are easy creatures to care for and fascinating to watch. Pet tarantulas need only a little water and a live insect, such as a cricket, to eat once a week. They are not noisy or dirty. Their cages might need cleaning once each year or even less often. No wonder they make popular pets!

Unfortunately, it is very difficult to raise baby tarantulas for pets in the same way that hamsters or goldfish are raised. This means pet tarantulas must be collected from the wild. If too many are taken, there may not be enough left to keep their numbers steady in the wild.

Medicines and Myths

Today, scientists are experimenting to see if the tarantula's poison can be used to make medicines.

Ever since ancient times, humans believed that tarantulas were useful in treating or preventing diseases. At one time, people placed tarantulas in nutshells and hung these on necklaces. They believed these necklaces would keep them from catching malaria, a terrible disease.

In parts of southeast Asia today, tarantulas are cut up and boiled with herbs to make a medicine. Swallowing this medicine is believed to be a cure for stomachaches.

Nearby, in Malaysia, no one would eat tarantulas. Here, they are called earth tigers and are thought to be messengers of the gods. Some Malaysians believe that people who hurt earth tigers will bring bad luck to themselves or their villages.

Tarantulas frighten and fascinate people all over the world. Although they are not as poisonous as many people think, they are amazing, and more is being learned about them all the time.

The underside view of this tarantula shows its two dark, curved fangs.

Chapter 2

A Closer Look

Tarantulas have been around on earth longer than any other kinds of spiders, and spiders have been around for 300 million years. One tarantula, preserved in a 40 million-year-old fossil, looks very much like the tarantulas alive today.

Tarantulas, like all spiders, are not insects. Insects have six legs. Spiders and their relatives, such as scorpions, ticks, and daddy longlegs, have eight legs. Tarantulas and all other spiders make up an **order**, or very large group of animals, called *Araneae*.

Tarantulas also belong to a smaller group of spiders known as *Mygalomorphs*. These animals all have fangs that point down. When a tarantula attacks a crawling insect, it pins the victim against the ground with its fangs. Spiders that aren't Mygalomorphs have fangs that point toward each other, like pinchers.

Spotlight on Species

Scientists believe that tarantulas spread far and wide when the continents were still connected, millions of years ago. Today, hundreds of different species live throughout the world. There are probably more undiscovered species in areas of South America and Africa.

About 30 species of tarantulas live in the United States. Most of them live in Arizona, Nevada, New Mexico, Texas, and the southern half of California. Others are found in Utah, Colorado, Kansas, Oklahoma, Missouri, Arkansas, and Louisiana. Some people have reported spotting tarantulas in Tennessee and in Florida, too.

Many of the tarantulas seen in the United

A brown tarantula.

States are simply called brown tarantulas because of their color. They live in burrows that they dig in deserts, grasslands, and woodlands throughout the southwest.

In southern Mexico, colorful Mexican red-knee tarantulas dig their burrows in the sides of

The Mexican red-knee.

hills. Because so many of these beautiful spiders were collected and sold for pets, they are now **endangered**. They may become **extinct**, or disappear from the earth, if they aren't protected. Mexico has passed laws to help save the red-knee, and collecting it is strictly controlled.

Many other species live in the tropical **rain forests** of Central and South America. They include the black velvet tarantula, the zebra tarantula, and the Brazilian pink-toe. The largest tarantula in the world, the Goliath bird-eater, lives here, too, in the forests of Brazil, Surinam, Guyana, and Venezuela.

In Africa, tarantulas are commonly called baboon spiders because their legs look like monkey fingers. Some Africans tell fortunes by studying the stripes and patterns on the baboon spider's body.

A Remarkable Body

Like all spiders, the tarantula's body is divided into two parts. The front, or head, is called the **cephalothorax**. The hard shell covering the cephalothorax is called the **carapace**. On top of the carapace are the tarantula's eyes, all eight of them. Even with eight eyes, the tarantula can't see

well at all. It cannot recognize objects more than a few feet away.

At the front of the tarantula's head are two pointed **chelicerae**, or jaws. The spider's mouth is hidden behind them. At the end of the jaws are the animal's fangs. The fangs in most species are about .5 inches (1.25 centimeters) long, and are connected to poison **glands** inside the jaws.

Eight legs extend from the cephalothorax. Each leg has seven joints. These jointed legs can move very quickly around and over objects. Many people believe that a tarantula can jump, but this is not true. Its body is too heavy for its legs to lift off the ground. Hairs at the end of the legs help the tarantula to grip smooth surfaces and to keep it from sinking into soft soil or sand.

Each leg also has two claws. The tarantula's sixteen claws help it cling to the sides of its burrow, or crawl up a rocky cliff or tree trunk.

Every tarantula has two long **pedipalps**, or

In this close-up of a Malaysian tarantula, its tiny eyes are visible on top of its carapace.

"foot feelers," by its jaws that are often mistaken for legs. A spider "tastes" things with its pedi-palps. Cells at the end of the "feelers" act like the taste buds on people's tongues. The spider can identify objects other than food, too, by touching them with its pedipalps.

The tarantula also feels with hairs that cover its body. These hairs sense even the tiniest of movements, such as an insect crawling on the ground nearby, or a moth flying through the air.

Behind the cephalothorax is the second part of the tarantula's body, the **abdomen**. Here, the spider's heart beats. It pumps like a human heart, but the blood is not inside veins or arteries. The pale, blue blood flows through an open-ended tube and out into the animal's tissues. If the tarantula's skin is broken, the spider can easily bleed to death.

The abdomen also contains the tarantula's lungs. The spider does not breathe in and out the way many animals do. Its lungs are called "book

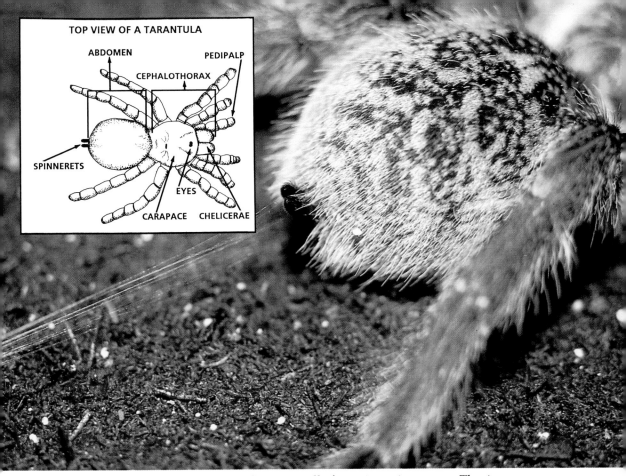

A South African tarantula spins silk from its spinnerets. The inset drawing shows the tarantula's spinnerets, as well as its other parts and organs.

lungs" because they are made up of many layers, like pages in a book. Air enters the lungs through openings in the abdomen. Then oxygen flows through the layers and is absorbed into the blood.

At the back of the abdomen are the spider's **spinnerets**. These glands contain many tiny tubes that release liquid silk. With this fine silk, the spider spins its thread.

A Slow Meal

Tarantulas, like all spiders, are **carnivores**. They eat animals rather than plants. Most of the time, they choose insects for their **prey**.

When a tarantula senses that an insect is near, it quickly runs to attack. Holding the prey still with its front legs, the spider stabs it with its fangs. Poison flows through the hollow fangs and into the insect, causing it to die. Then the tarantula crushes its prey with its jaws.

The spider's poison softens the inside of the insect's body. Now, juices pour from the spider's mouth and finish turning the insect's insides to liquid.

At last, the tarantula uses its powerful stomach muscles to suck the liquids from the insect's body. As the tarantula eats, hairs around its mouth trap hard pieces of its prey's broken shell.

The spider takes a break and walks around. Then it grasps the insect again, in a different spot, and continues to eat.

It will take the spider 20 minutes to several hours to eat. All that's left when the spider finishes is a lump of crushed shell or hard skin. Then the tidy tarantula cleans its jaws and the hairs around its mouth.

Tarantulas do not need to eat often. A single grasshopper may be enough food for two months. Tarantulas have survived more than two years on water alone. Beetles and crickets are the most common food because there are so many and they are easy to find. But what the tarantula chooses to eat depends on its size and where it lives.

Tarantulas live in rain forests—such as this one in Costa Rica—as well as many other habitats on earth.

Chapter 3

Tarantulas at Home

Tarantulas live in many different **habitats**. They are found in deserts, woodlands, and rain forests. Some species even live high in mountains, such as the Andes of South America and the Himalayas of Asia.

In dry climates, such as the southwestern United States, tarantulas build their homes underground—in hillsides, beneath rocks, or in termite mounds. They dig their burrows with their jaws and move the clumps of dirt with their pedipalps. The hard-working tarantula digs its burrow straight down for nearly 1 foot (30 centimeters), and then sideways for 1 or 2 feet (30 or 60 centimeters).

Some species pile dirt, pebbles, leaves, and twigs at the entrance to their burrows. The spiders sit on these mounds, warming their bodies in the sunshine and waiting for their prey. But most of the time, they sit inside their burrows instead of outside. If you point a flashlight into a tarantula's burrow, you may see the spider's eight eyes shining back at you.

Some tarantulas line the inside of their burrows with silk. The silk lining acts like a net that keeps the dirt walls from caving in and filling the burrow. Silk threads around the entrance also tell the tarantula when prey is nearby. When an insect touches the threads, the movement travels down the silk lining to the hungry spider below.

In Central and South America, and in other tropical areas, too, some species of tarantulas live in trees instead of in burrows. They build their homes—tube-shaped webs—in branches or in hollow trunks. Others live closer to the ground, in

A tarantula and its silk burrow are visible inside an old, fallen log in the rain forest of Trinidad Island.

fallen logs or between the leaves of low-growing plants.

Tarantulas that live in tropical regions are the largest of all the species. They eat the largest prey, too. Certain species are called bird-eaters because they sometimes eat baby birds in their nests. But, like other tarantulas, they mainly eat insects.

Dangers and Defenses

All tarantulas, no matter where they live, have enemies in nature. Some of their **predators**, or animals that hunt them for food, are lizards, birds, frogs, skunks, raccoons, and coyotes. The coatimundi, a Central and South American relative of the raccoon, eats many tarantulas.

Another enemy is the ant. Ants enter tarantulas' burrows and eat baby spiders and eggs. There is nothing tarantulas can do to fight them. Ants are too small for the spiders to bite.

In Texas, one species of tarantula allows tiny

This Goliath bird-eater lives in tropical French Guiana.

toads to share its home underground. The toads help the spider by eating any ants that come into the burrow. In return, if a snake comes into the burrow looking for a toad to eat, the tiny toads hide under the giant spider.

The tarantula scares the snake away by threatening to bite or by "kicking hairs." By rubbing its back pair of legs against its abdomen, the tarantula flings thousands of hairs into the air. These hairs are **barbed** with tiny, sharp hooks that irritate the enemy's nose, mouth, and eyes. Sometimes they cause a painful rash or even blindness in the attacking animal. A bald spot on a tarantula's abdomen is a sign that it has been kicking hairs.

Kicking hairs won't always scare away a predator, but the tarantula doesn't give up. When an enemy catches it by a leg, the leg simply breaks off, and the spider scurries away. It moves quite easily on seven legs. But even so, it will grow a new leg to replace the lost one within a year.

Losing a leg, kicking hairs, or biting usually cannot help a tarantula in fighting its worst enemy, the tarantula hawk wasp. This blue-black wasp crawls over the ground, exploring with its long antenna. When it finds the spider's burrow,

A tarantula hawk wasp attacks a Chilean tarantula.

it disturbs the silk threads around the entrance. The tarantula climbs out of the burrow, expecting to find a meal. Instead, it finds a deadly enemy.

Instantly, the tarantula rises on its hind legs to bite with its long fangs. This is a mistake. The wasp can now sting under the spider's abdomen, the one spot where the wasp's poison works.

The wasp's poison does not kill the spider, but paralyzes it. The wasp digs a grave 8 inches (20 centimeters) deep, and drags the spider, 10 times its weight, into the grave. Then the wasp lays an egg on the spider's abdomen, and buries them together. When the egg hatches, the wasp **larva** feeds on the spider. The spider lives for weeks in this condition, and at last, dies.

Unfriendly Neighbors

Sometimes, as many as 20 tarantulas may live close together on a warm, sunny hillside. But they don't live as neighbors on purpose or because they are friendly. In fact, tarantulas, like all spiders, are **cannibals** and will eat their own kind. They might just turn a visiting spider into a good meal.

Tarantulas' homes are close together because **spiderlings**, or baby tarantulas, walk away from their nests instead of parachuting on the breeze as many spiders do. They don't go far before settling down. Females may spend their entire lives in the same burrow. Males live in the same burrows until, as adults, they travel to find mates.

Chapter 4

The Tarantula's Year

In warm regions, tarantulas stay active year-round. In colder climates, the spiders take a long rest for the winter. They don't hibernate, like bears. Instead, they plug the entrances to their burrows with soil, and rest without eating for several months.

About March, the tarantulas come out of their burrows. At first, they simply sit and warm themselves in the sunlight. These are cold-blooded animals. Their bodies do not make heat like birds and mammals do. Tarantulas raise their body temperature to a comfortable level by resting in the sun.

After a few days, the spiders begin to eat and

This Brazilian pink-toe tarantula rests in the sun to raise its body temperature.

make home repairs. The winter rains tore the silk linings and washed dirt into the holes. Now, the spiders remove the dirt and line the burrows with new silk. Soon, strengthened by a few meals, they are ready for an active summer.

Eggs and Spiderlings

In warm climates, the female lays her eggs a few months after mating. In cool climates, she waits until her winter rest is over. She begins by weaving a clean sheet of silk. This sometimes takes several hours.

When she finishes the weaving, the female lays many eggs on the silk sheet. Depending on her species, she lays 100 to 1000 eggs. She then spins a silk cover and draws the sheet around the eggs. The female wraps the bundle with more silk and rolls it around until it is shaped like a ball. This is the tarantula's **cocoon**. Sometimes it is as large as a golf ball.

A female Mexican red-knee lays her eggs on a silk sheet. To the scientist, the pool of eggs looks like a bowl of tapioca pudding.

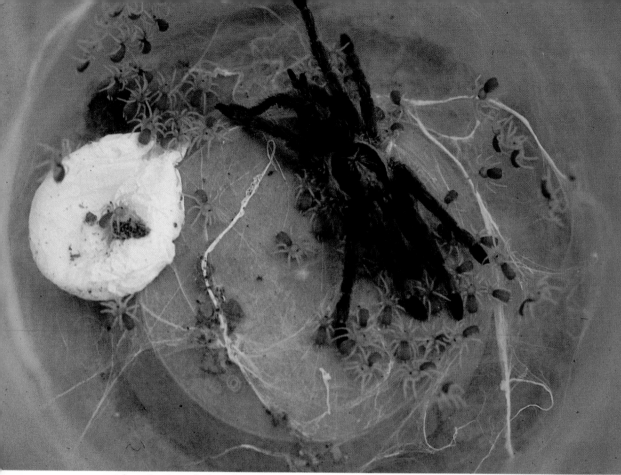

After the female lays her eggs, many weeks pass before her spiderlings hatch and leave the cocoon.

The female keeps the cocoon with her in the burrow. At times, she drags it outside to warm, but she never strays more than one or two feet from it. She is always ready to defend her eggs. If an enemy threatens them, the female stands near with her fangs spread wide, ready to attack.

In about four to six weeks, the eggs hatch. The spiderlings stay safely inside the cocoon for about five more weeks. Finally, they chew a few holes in the silk ball, and hundreds of spiderlings parade into the world. It may take two days for all of them to leave the cocoon.

Baby tarantulas look like their parents, although they are much smaller and lighter in color. After hatching, they stay near their mother for less than a week. If they remain any longer, they risk being eaten by their mother, brothers, or sisters.

Molting

Soon after the spiderlings leave, the female **molts**, or sheds, her skin. She, like all spiders, has a hard shell on the outside of her body. This shell, called an **exoskeleton**, is similar to a suit of armor. It protects the organs and tissues inside her. An exoskeleton does not grow. It must be shed for the

45

animal inside to continue growing. Underneath her old shell, the female has a new shell ready to take its place.

Before a tarantula molts, it stops eating and moves around very little. The spider turns on its back, and the carapace splits open. Pushing and pulling, the spider frees itself from its old shell. It wiggles its legs to keep them from becoming stiff as the new exoskeleton hardens. Molting takes about an hour. But it can take as long as 24 hours from the time the spider begins to molt until it is up on its feet again.

Molting is a dangerous time for the tarantula. Its new shell is too soft to protect the spider from predators. A tear in its new exoskeleton may cause the animal to bleed to death. The tarantula loses its sense of sight and touch while molting and its lungs stop working for a while. Tarantulas should not be handled during molting.

However dangerous, molting has advantages

This tarantula is shedding its exoskeleton.

for the spider. It grows all new hair, covering any bald spots from kicking hairs. The tarantula also grows new legs where old ones broke off during battles or in accidents.

Baby tarantulas molt more than four times while they are still inside the cocoon. They will

Four tarantulas have shed their exoskeletons and left behind their old, empty shells.

molt several more times in each of the first two years after hatching. Every year after this, they molt just once or twice.

Some species of tarantulas become adults within a few years. The more common species in the United States and in Mexico take about 10 to

12 years to grow up. It is difficult to tell males from females until the males molt for the last time. When this happens, their legs grow longer, and their carapaces become a brighter color. Their pedipalps now have bulb-shaped tips that they will use in mating.

Finding a Mate

When they are full-grown, male tarantulas of many species leave their burrows. In the southwestern United States, it is common to see them wandering from late August to early November. They march over hillsides and across highways, searching for females.

During this time of searching, many males are killed by predators or run over by cars. The lucky ones stay alive and find a female's burrow at last.

The male sits patiently outside the female's burrow, sometimes waiting for days until she appears. Or he might tap on the silk lining like a

The male (on the right) taps the female (on the left) with his legs.

knock on the door. When the female climbs out, the male is careful not to be mistaken for a tasty meal. He taps the female with his legs. This seems to tell her that he is another tarantula, and not breakfast or lunch.

This tapping appears to calm the female and

keep her from attacking. She rises on her hind legs, and the male catches her fangs with special hooks on his front legs. Now, he can mate without being bitten.

Many people believe that the female kills and eats the male, but this is rarely the case. Most of the time, the male wanders off after mating and may even find another female to mate again. But the male's life work is now done, and he won't live much longer. Usually, he dies of old age a few months later.

The Tarantula's Future

Every year, more tarantulas are born and some die. If they were left alone, their species would continue to survive. But today, their population may be threatened. Collecting too many tarantulas for pets is just one threat.

Cities in the southwestern United States grow larger every day. As more roads, houses, and freeways are built, there is less land for tarantulas to dig their burrows. Destroying their habitat is the worst threat to these giant spiders.

In tropical regions of the world, thousands of acres of rain forest are destroyed each day. Millions of trees are cut down to make room for farming and ranching. For tarantulas and other tropical animals, this means disaster. Many species of animals and plants are becoming extinct.

Pesticides, or poisons used to kill insects, also harm many tarantulas. They can die after being sprayed with poison, or after eating a poisoned insect.

Humans threaten the tarantula's survival in many ways. Should we change our actions to save this remarkable animal and its habitat? Yes, but why? Tarantulas and other spiders are a very important part of nature. They help to keep nature in balance by eating insects that eat plants. This helps the plants to grow. Without spiders, people and other animals would have trouble finding enough plants to eat. Spiders are an important part of the food chain, too. They serve as food for many other animals.

Some scientists believe that humans could not survive without the help of spiders. One scientist estimates that if every spider ate 100 insects during its lifetime, then the insects that spiders eat each year would weigh more than all the human beings on earth.

Tarantulas are good neighbors. They are quiet and useful, and they don't cause any damage. We must be sure to protect these remarkable spiders and their habitat, to help them survive far into the future.

Glossary

abdomen (AB-duh-muhn)—back section on a spider's body

barbed—having barbs; a barb is a sharp point that is attached to an object and sticks out backwards; fish hooks and arrows have barbs

cannibal (KAN-ih-buhl)—a person or animal that eats the flesh of its own kind

carapace (KAIR-uh-pays)—the hard covering on the cephalothorax of a spider's body

carnivore (KAR-nih-vohr)—a flesh-eating animal

cephalothorax (SEF-uh-luh-THAWR-aks)—the front section of a spider's body

chelicerae (kuh-LIHS-uh-ruh)—a spider's jaws; used for grasping and crushing; the fangs are attached to the chelicerae

cocoon (kuh-KOON)—a case made out of silk that contains insect eggs; protects the eggs until they develop and hatch

endangered—an animal or plant having a population so low that it is in danger of becoming extinct

exoskeleton (EHKS-oh-SKEHL-uh-tuhn)—the hard skin or shell on many boneless animals, such as insects and spiders

extinct (ehk-STINGKT)—no longer living anywhere on earth; many plant and animal species have become extinct

gland—an organ that makes materials needed by the body for special purposes, such as sweat

habitat (HAB-ih-tat)—the region where a plant or animal naturally lives

larva (LAHR-vuh)—the young of an insect that looks unlike the parent and that must change before becoming an adult

molt—to shed an outer layer, such as skin or a shell, before it is replaced with a new outer layer

nocturnal (nock-TURN-uhl)—active during the night

order—a group of related people, animals, or things; all spiders belong to the same order

pedipalps (PEHD-uh-palpz)—a pair of leg-like "feelers" on a spider's cephalothorax; used to identify objects and to hold food

pesticide (PES-tuh-syde)—poison used to destroy insects

predator (PREHD-uh-tuhr)—an animal that hunts other animals for food

prey—an animal that is hunted by another animal for food

rain forest—a dense, humid tropical forest; occurs in areas that have high rainfall throughout the year

species (SPEE-sheez)—distinct kinds of individual plants or animals that have common characteristics and share a common name

spiderling—a baby spider

spinnerets (spin-uh-REHTS)—glands on a spider's abdomen that release liquid silk

venom (VEHN-uhm)—the poison that certain animals can pass to their enemies through a bite or a sting

About the Author

At her house near San Francisco, Gail LaBonte often watches tarantulas march across her yard. Close to home, she hikes frequently on Mount Diablo, where she observes tarantulas, too. Ms. LaBonte is an elementary school teacher in Berkeley, California, where she shares her knowledge of tarantulas and her love for all animals with her students. The author is a member of the Society of Children's Book Writers. She is also the author of *The Llama, The Artic Fox,* and *The Miniature Horse,* three other Dillon Remarkable Animals books. Ms. LaBonte lives in Danville, California, with her husband and two children.